Fennec Foxes:

Wily Desert Hunters

*The **My Favorite Animals** Series*

Claire Johnston

Fennec Foxes: Wily Desert Hunters

(The My Favorite Animals Series)

Copyright 2013 Bonnie L. Johnston

Open Clearing Press

ISBN-13: 978-1494351748

ISBN-10: 1494351749

This book is dedicated to
Layden Drake Johnston,
who's even cuter
than a fennec fox.

To thank you for buying this book, I'd like to give you a free e-book.

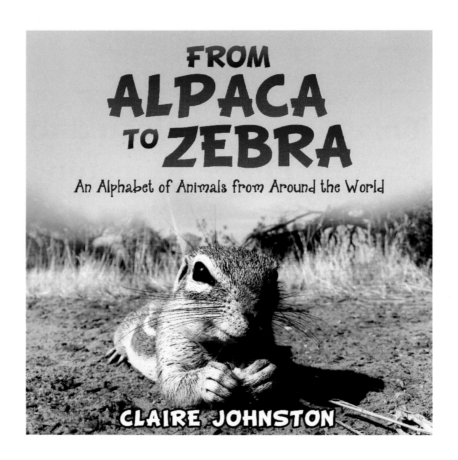

To receive your free e-book, go to:
freebook.authorclairejohnston.com

Table of Contents

What Kind of Animal is a Fennec Fox?

Fennec foxes are members of the canid family. They are related to dogs and wolves.

They are often called "desert foxes," because they live in deserts.

What Do They Look Like?

Fennec foxes have big, bat-like ears. They have very good hearing—they can hear rodents and insects under the ground.

Their ears also help them stay cool during the day. There are lots of little hairs in their ears to keep sand and insects out.

Their fur is sand-colored, so they are good at hiding in the desert. They may have dark markings on their muzzles and on the tips of their ears. It can be freezing cold at night in the desert, so their fur is very thick.

Fennec foxes have fur on their paws that keeps them from getting burned when they walk on hot sand. They also have bristles on their paws which help them grip loose sand more easily.

Fennec foxes are about the same size as Chihuahuas. They weigh about two to three pounds.

Where Do They Live?

Fennec foxes live in the deserts of North Africa and the Middle East. You might meet a fennec fox if you visit Egypt or Nigeria. You can also find them in Kuwait and Morocco.

It is very hot in the desert during the day, so fennec foxes sleep during the day and hunt at night.

What Are Their Homes Like?

Fennec foxes live in underground dens that they dig. They love to dig—a fennec fox can dig a twenty foot hole in one night.

A fennec fox's den can be bigger than a football field, and can have more than a dozen doors for the fennec to go in and out.

They often dig their dens at the base of sand dunes, where the soil is moister. That moisture helps keep the fennec's den cool even during the hottest part of the day.

Sometimes two or more fennec families will connect their dens by digging tunnels between them.

What Sounds Do They Make?

Fennec foxes make many different sounds. Sometimes they bark or yap. Sometimes they purr like a cat. When a fennec fox is scared, it snarls.

Fennec foxes may squeak or squeal when they are excited or happy, and they wag their tails like dogs. They also make whining sounds like dogs.

What Do They Eat?

Fennec foxes eat lots of insects, especially grasshoppers and locusts.

Grasshopper

African Locust

They also like rodents, lizards, birds, and eggs. Sometimes they eat the leaves or roots of plants, or fruits and berries.

They can go for a long time without water. They drink dew and they drink water when they can find it, but they get most of their liquids from the plants they eat.

Since they eat both plants and other animals, fennec foxes are omnivores. Omnivore means "eats everything."

When fennec foxes catch extra food, they may store it to eat later.

How Do They Hunt?

Fennec foxes can jump two feet up and four feet forward. They are fast and can change direction easily. This makes them good at catching mice and lizards.

They also have sensitive noses which let them sniff out prey—and danger.

Sometimes they have to dig for their dinner. If you see a fennec staring at the ground, moving its ears back and forth, it is listening for a mouse that is hiding underground.

What Are Their Families Like?

A fennec family is made up of a mother fennec, a father fennec, and all of their children. Older children stay with their mother and father even after newer children are born.

A mother fennec has between two and five babies at a time. A baby fox is called a cub. When it is born, a cub weighs about an ounce and its eyes are sealed shut. They are usually born at the end of winter or the beginning of spring.

Cubs stay underground with their mother until they are ten weeks old. The mother fennec nurses her cubs for one to three months. After it is one month old, a cub can eat food that its parents catch.

The father fennec protects the mother and cubs, and brings them food. Once a mother and father fennec pair up to start a family, they stay together for the rest of their lives.

Fennec foxes are adults when they are nine months old. They can live for ten to fourteen years.

How Do They Play?

Play time for fennec foxes is practice for hunting. Young ones chase each other and pounce on each other like cats do. They love to wrestle. And they love to dig.

What Are They Afraid Of?

Animals that hunt fennec foxes include African eagle owls, desert lynxes called caracals, jackals, hyenas, and a kind of dog called a "saluki".

African spotted eagle owl   Caracal

Jackal   Hyena

Domesticated Saluki

Sometimes people hunt fennec foxes for their beautiful cream-colored fur.

A fennec fox's hearing is so good that it can usually hear dangerous animals coming and hide in its den.

How Are They Different From Other Foxes?

Fennec foxes are the smallest type of fox, but their ears are bigger than any other fox's ears.

Fennec fox   European red fox

Other foxes have musk glands that give off a strong smell, but fennec foxes do not have musk glands, so they do not smell like other foxes.

Other foxes live alone, but fennec foxes can live in packs of up to ten members.

Some scientists think that even though fennec foxes look similar to other foxes, they are their own special kind of animal.

Fun Facts: Did You Know?

The fennec fox is the national animal of Algeria. The Algerian soccer team is named after these foxes: they call themselves "Les Fennecs."

The Pokemon named Fennekin is based on the fennec fox.

Conclusion

Fennec foxes are a unique species. They are hard to study in the wild, so most of what we have learned about them comes from watching them in zoos.

It takes a lot of work to get close enough to take a picture of a wild fennec fox, because they can hear you coming with those big, adorable ears!

I'm so happy to have shared this information about fennec foxes with you!

For links to videos of fennec foxes and information about my other children's books, please visit:

www.authorclairejohnston.com

I look forward to seeing you there!

Claire

Made in the USA
Columbia, SC
14 December 2018